HOW
I TRAINED
MY COLT

by Sandy Rabinowitz

SCHOLASTIC INC.
New York Toronto London Auckland Sydney

ISBN 0-590-32513-2

12 11 10 9 8 7 6 5 4 3 2   5 6 7 8 9/8 0/9

Printed in the U.S.A.

28

Dear Readers,

This is a story about training a horse. A young girl tells the story. She is a lot like me when I was young.

I have owned horses since I was eight years old. I began to train horses by asking other horse owners how to do it.

I also read many books about training horses.

I have raised three foals, or baby horses. Their names are Sunset, Calico, and Sunny. Sunny is the horse in this book.

Sandy Rabinowitz

Sunny had just been born.

I wanted to make friends with him.

I tried to pet him.

But Sunny hid behind

his mother, Sundance.

He was scared.

I did not want to frighten him.

I sat in the corner and watched him.

Soon he came over to look at me.

He sniffed my sweater,

my hair, and my nose.

He licked my cheek.

Sunny's nose was soft.

His whiskers tickled.

I slowly put out a hand.

He sniffed it.

Then I scratched him on the neck.

He liked that.

For the next few days,

I spent all of my time with Sunny.

I watched him in the field.

He ran and jumped and kicked.

When he was hungry,

he drank milk from Sundance.

When he was tired, he took naps.

Although Sunny and I were friends,

he had to learn that I was the boss.

I wanted to ride him when he grew up.

So he had to learn to obey me.

He was only two days old.

I was bigger and stronger

than he was.

But in only two weeks he would be

bigger and stronger than I.

It was time for Sunny's first lesson.

I put one arm around his chest.

I put the other arm

around his rump.

Sunny tried to get away.

I held on tight

and talked softly to him.

Soon he stood still.

Then I patted him and let him go. 11

Horses learn by doing things
over and over again.
They learn by being rewarded.
I held Sunny many times.
As a reward,
I always patted him
when he stood still.
He learned that I
was his friend *and* his boss.

When Sunny was a week old,

I put a halter on him.

He did not like wearing it.

He tried to take it off.

For the next few days

I put on Sunny's halter

for fifteen minutes at a time.

Soon he was used to wearing it.

Sunny was growing fast.

If the halter was too tight,

I loosened it.

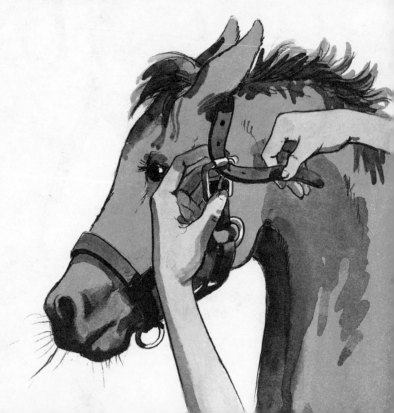

When Sunny was two weeks old,

it was time to train him

to follow me while I led him.

I asked my brother Mike to help.

I told Mike to lead Sundance,

Sunny's mother.

Sunny followed his mother.

I walked beside Sunny.

I said, "Walk on," to him

as we walked.

We did this for a few minutes.

Then I tried to lead Sunny

without following Sundance.

I said, "Walk on."

He would not move.

I did not want to pull him forward.

I did not want a tug-of-war.

Sunny could easily win that.

Instead, I put a rope
around his rump.

I said, "Walk on."

He did not move.

I tugged on the rope.

Sunny jumped forward!

He was a good boy.

As a reward,

I hugged him and let him go.

After a few more lessons,
Sunny was easy to lead.
Then he was ready
to learn something new.
It was time to teach him
to be tied up.
I tied him to a strong tree
with a slip knot.

He tried to walk away.

He couldn't!

He was scared

and he was mad.

He pulled and pulled.

I talked to Sunny
to calm him down.
When he stopped fighting
and stood still,
I rewarded him
by patting him.
Then I let him go.

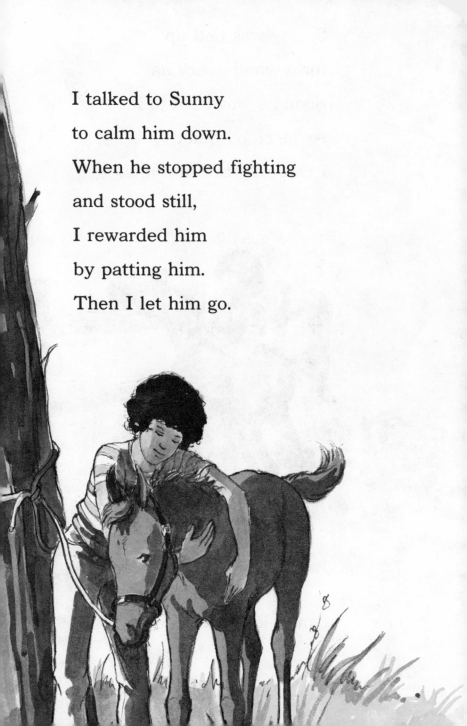

Sunny was tied up
for a while every day.
Soon he was used to it.
As he stood quietly,
I carefully brushed him.

Sunny loved this lesson.

By the time Sunny
was one month old,
he had learned a lot.
But he still had to learn
good manners.
Most of the time
Sunny was gentle and friendly.
But sometimes he was too playful.

I wasn't strong enough

or fast enough

to "horse around" with him.

I had to yell, "No!"

Sometimes I had to spank

Sunny on the rump.

When Sunny was six months old,

he was not a baby anymore.

He had grown over a foot taller.

He had gained 400 lbs (200 kgs).

He was ready to leave his mother.

I put him in a field
with a pony named Smoky.

Smoky and Sunny

had a lot of fun that winter.

At last spring came.

Every day, I went

riding on Sundance.

We took Sunny along.

Sunny loved to play

on these rides.

He liked to gallop past us
as fast as he could.

Then he would wait ahead.
We would ride past him.

Then he would gallop up from behind
and pass us again.

Sunny also played "road hog."
He liked to get in front of us
and go slowly.
He would not let us pass him!

Sunny was smart.
He learned things
as he played.
He learned to cross streams.

He learned to jump stone walls.

He learned that many kinds
of animals live in the woods.

If something scared Sunny,

I rode Sundance past it.

Then Sunny would see

that there was nothing to fear.

May 17 was
Sunny's birthday.
He was one year old.
Now he was ready
for harder lessons.
I wanted to teach Sunny
to walk, trot, and stop
on command.
Again Mike helped me.
We led Sunny
to a flat part of the field.

I put a long rope
on Sunny's halter.
This rope is called a "lunge line."
I let Sunny sniff the whip
I was holding.

Then I asked Mike to lead
Sunny around me in a circle.
I said, "Walk on."
Mike led him forward.
I said, "Whoa."
Mike stopped him.

Then I told Mike
to let go of the halter
and walk beside Sunny.
Again I said, "Walk on."
Sunny knew he wasn't being led.
He did not know what to do.
He turned and tried to walk to me.

I pointed the whip at him

to keep him away.

But Sunny was not afraid of it.

He wanted to play tug-of-war

with the whip.

Mike led him back onto the circle.

I said, "Walk on."

Sunny tried to turn to me again.

I cracked the whip loudly

right behind him.

Boy, did he jump!

At last he understood.

He walked forward quickly.

Then I said, "Whoa."

He stopped right away.

I patted Sunny

and gave him a carrot.

I had taught Sunny to walk and stop

on the lunge line.

This is called "lunging"

a horse.

Mike helped me lunge Sunny

for the next few days.

Sunny was easy to train

if we rewarded him

when he was good.

He loved to be patted.

He liked to be told

how wonderful he was.

That is why he tried to please us.

By December, Sunny
looked big and powerful.
But he still acted like a foal,
a baby horse.

That winter, I gave Sunny
a rest.
He had learned his lessons well.
I was proud of him.

When the snow melted, I began
to train him again.
I wanted to ride Sunny.
He had to learn to wear
a saddle, a bridle, and a bit.

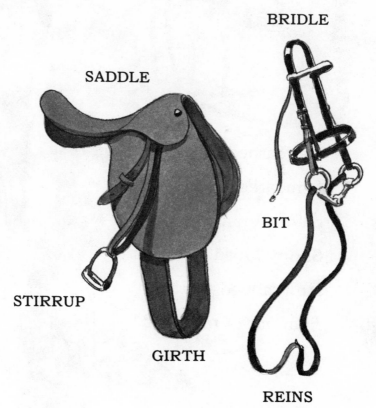

SADDLE

BRIDLE

BIT

STIRRUP

GIRTH

REINS

He learned to wear the bit first.

I smeared molasses on it

before I put it on him.

Sunny loved molasses.

He grabbed the bit

right out of my hand.

For the next few days,
I let Sunny wear
the bit and bridle
a little longer each time.
When Sunny was used to them,
he was ready for the saddle.
I put the saddle on the fence.
Then I led him up to it.

He was a little scared of it.

He seemed ready to run away

if it moved.

It did not, so Sunny sniffed it.

He decided that it was safe.

I tied Sunny up.

Then I carried the saddle to him.

I carefully placed it on his back.

Sunny did not mind having it there.

So I buckled it on.

Sunny was a very good boy!

Every day for a week I lunged
Sunny with the saddle
and bridle on.
He looked like a grown-up horse,
but he was not ready to ride yet.
Before I could ride him,
he had to learn to obey the reins.

A pull on the right rein
means turn right.
A pull on the left rein
means turn left.
A pull on both reins at once
means slow down or stop.

To teach him
to obey the reins,
I tied a long rope
to each side of the bit.
I stood behind Sunny
and held on to the ropes.

Mike led Sunny forward.

I followed behind.

I said, "Walk on."

Then I pulled softly
on the left rope.
Sunny felt this pull.
He turned left,
as I had asked.
But he turned too much.

I straightened him out
by pulling on the right rein.

Then I tried to keep him
walking in a straight line.
At first it was hard.
Sunny zigzagged
all over the place.

But after a few lessons

I could drive him well.

Then he was ready to be ridden.

I picked a warm, sunny day.

First I lunged Sunny.

Then I asked Mike to hold him still.

Slowly, I pulled myself up.

I talked softly all the while.

I wanted Sunny to be calm.

At first, I lay across the saddle.
I wanted Sunny to get
used to my weight.
Then I asked Mike to lead him
slowly forward.

Sunny was not scared.

But he was wobbly.

He was not used to carrying

a person on his back.

I asked Mike to stop Sunny.

I pulled myself up

and sat in the saddle.

I looked down
at the pointy brown ears
in front of me.
I was really up there
at last!

I told Mike to walk
close beside me.
I said, "Walk on."
Sunny walked!

I pulled on the left rein.

Sunny turned!

He had learned
his lessons well.
I remembered when Sunny
was born.
He was very tiny and timid.
Now he was big and strong!
I could ride him!
We had both grown
and learned so much.